Life, love, loss and all the feelings between

Roxanne Noonan

BookLeaf Publishing

Life, love, loss and all the feelings between

Presentation by *BookLeaf Publishing*

Web: www.bookleafpub.com

E-mail: info@bookleafpub.com

ISBN: 9789357213165

First edition 2023

This book is dedicated to the following;
My daughter Zoe you are the light in my dark; you give me hope when I feel none you give me purpose in life.
Zoe - I never knew what love was until I met you, and I am forever greatful and thankful that the universe sent you to me.

I would also like to dedicate this book to my Grandfather, Bob.
I thank you for your talents; your love of art and the written word. I'm thankful daily for this beautiful creative gift that you passed on to me. Your love of life, hard work and dedication in life have always been inspirational to me and hopefully my children's lives too... I'm so proud to be your Grandaughter.

To my mother and my father, for always loving me and letting me grow through experiences in life.
Thank you for always loving me, no matter how difficult or strange I could be growing up. Your love was really all I needed to flourish, and I've always felt so loved by you both.

To my loving husband, my quiet supporter.
Thank you for allowing me to feel through my rawness and encouraging me to embrace my

wild, free, and sometimes firey nature. You have supported this book from conception to birth, and I can't thank you enough.

To my best friend Danni, my hype woman.
Thank you for pushing me through this writing process and encouraging me, even when I felt like giving up.

To my friends and loved ones... and the one that needs no mention by name... Thank you for supporting me throughout this, I thank you from the bottom of my heart. This has been a wild and emotional ride, full of highs and a bunch of lows... Thank you for a lifetime of inspiration, love, support and encouragement - I will honour that for a lifetime.

I truly love you all from the bottom of my heart.

Queen of the night

The heat of the South African months
beautiful and dry
Like no other;
The sounds, the smells
Are fond to me,
The summers hold special memories.

My father would wake me
to gaze upon the Queen of the night.
How magical, this cactus,
that the flower would be gone by daylight.

The smell;
I remember it like yesterday;
Soft and sweet;
This white beauty.

How can something so painful
Be so magical?

My father,
like me,
loved nature in all its raw beauty;
Lightning storms in all their glory.

He'd let the wind rush through the windows,
howling, whipping up the room.
He'd smile as we clung to him in gleeful fear, oh
how I remember those storms in those magical
hours.

My father would star gaze for hours..
in the clear South Africa skies, he told me how
magical and special they are!

Now I'm older, I miss these things
but my father shares
the talks of the moon and the stars
with my littlest one.

My father, he loved the South African land.
It's in his blood;
It's in mine too..
It's part of my daughters blood and memories
now too.

Lantana

Between the paper bark trees,
The lantana weaves it way through the landscape;
Its dense and deep,
climbing deeper and deeper.
The beautiful lantana Flowers,
blooming hues of pink and yellow;
Enticing inviting.

It reminds me of toxic love;
It's beauty bewildering, it's so easy to forget it's potent at best.
It's beautiful and devastating,
It's dense and hard to remove -
They call it a knoxious weed..but its beautiful too.
How can something so beautiful be so bad?
Something so strong
Be banned from the land?

Lantana weaves between the trees
Impeding, imprinting it's very own soul.
The Lantana has a place in my heart..
It's beautiful,
It's poison;

It captured my imagination.

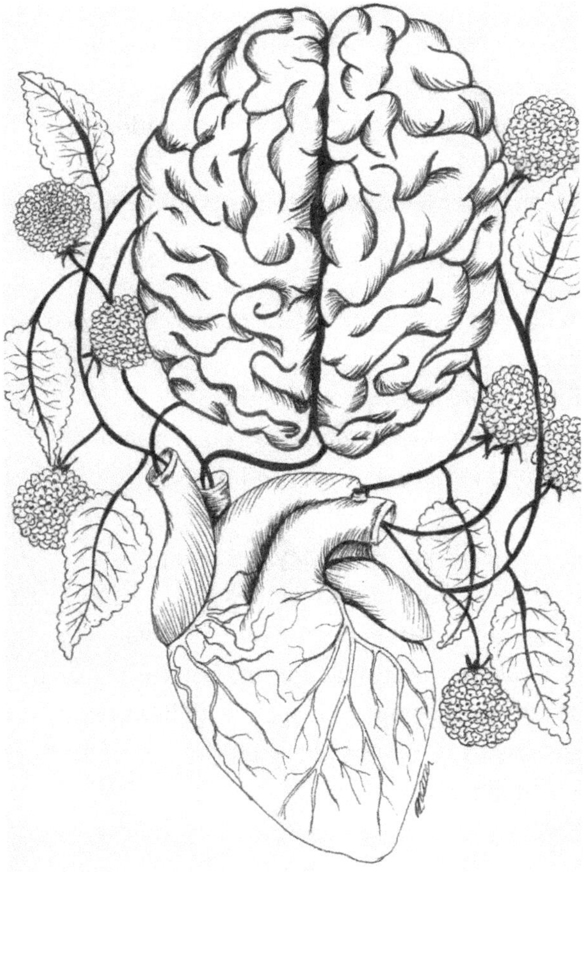

Weeds

Weeds grew from her mouth, with every lie, a
new seed spouted.
The weeds grew deeper and wove within her
heart,
Taking over her entire being, invading every part
of her.

With every word she spoke, the weeds inched
deeper,
Enveloping her very soul
Taking over her beauty, covering her until she
had nothing else but lies, and lies..

The tendrils grab onto any lost soul,
Her thorns cutting into the flesh...
Dragging you both deeper into the abyss..
With every sprout that appears solidifying your
destiny into complete dispair with her toxicity.
Eventually there is nothing left;
You don't look like you,
You can't recognise yourself.
Weeds killing every part of her body, invading
her, devouring her soul..and now she's here for
you.

She was no more,
And she needed you.
She was no more,
And needed the strength and beauty of you.
She was no more,
So now she takes you.

The only solution to end it all;
Poison you both, and
Die and wither away.

War inside me

Therapist to all but me;
No time to cry,
No time to be.
At night,
A magical time between
Sleep and isolation,
I hear my heartbeat.
Sadness sets in;
My optimism
Armour...
You don't see the war,
You think you see me,
You don't see the places I'm lost,
You don't see the war inside of me.
Therapist to others
Fighting your battles;
Wiping tears
Fears of others,
Then as the night descends,
I tuck myself in
Alone again in my mind
Alone as the tears unfold
Enveloping where I lie.

I'll wake up in the morning,
I'll smile;
You'll never know...
Forever the optimst,
Forever in someone else's mind,
Forever my own comfort
In my own head...
My heart, it cried to be seen
but I kept smiling...
I'll ask if you're okay then tuck myself in...
Alone again in my mind.

Shadow

You broke me,
You tried to change me,
You blamed me.
You were the shadow looming behind me;
Waiting for me.
You hunted me,
You loved to hurt me,
Why?
You were a shadow
I had one..
But your shadow, it scared me.
You had me, but it was never enough.
You said you loved me
But how could you hurt me?
You were a shadow that stood over me,
A shadow that marked me,
Forever changed me,
You bruised me,
You scarred me,
Standing over me,
Intimidating me,
A shadow that blamed me,
Lied about me,
Broke me
Then laughed

While you tortured me.
Your shadow stood over me
Until I couldn't stand it.
Your shadow kept me dark too long.
Your shadow screamed the day I let in the light;
Your shadow lurked.. for years to come.
Your shadow tried to devour me
But you failed to find me.
Your shadow, no longer mine but someone
else's;
The burden of leaving, knowing you'll stand
over another.
Your shadow, never mine.
Your shadow is gone,
Your shadow, just a history -
Never to stand where I stand.

Butterfly

I had been through unimaginable things
I'd never dream about meeting you..
The universe alignment, perfect that night..
I'm so greatful for you.

Your smile so radiant,
You so calm
You made me laugh, and smile
like never before;
I, the mess waking from the storm.
Post traumatic stress disorder;
A shadow still looming behind me...
Living in fear.

You came to me,
You loved me and delighted in me,
You gave me kindness
Reminding me.. this is how it should feel!
You showed me back myself;
You showed such kindness and tenderness.

I wasn't always a delight,
No one gave you credit.
I was hard to love;
I was broken too.

You gave me everything in that moment, You saved my life... You just never knew!

You showed me..
I was worthy of love.
You reminded me how strong I could be in the face of adversity.
You set me free in many ways;
You let me sleep in my cocoon,
Holding me when it got too hard.

You allowed my wings to grow and expand in a new and wonderful world.
You helped me shed my old skin,
You walked with me into the light without the dark.
You called me your butterfly...
Thank you for loving me and allowing my true self to fly free.

Journey

To want something so much,
No guarentees.
The times we tried and failed,
My journey filled with tears and fears.
Three times
Down this road.

The physical pain, barely a flinch.
With every needle, a hope sets in
Behind my smile..
I hope and prayed
I wait and wait
I think of names
Pondered on boy or girl.
The want,
The despair,
Then that call unbearable!

The water I wash in turns crimson once again,
The tears down my face;
I hide, knowing I have to do this again.
The pain of it all,
The hurt it causes me,
The toll on us,
The failure I feel.

How can I be a woman
If this is what I am?
I've asked myself a millions times;
I've screamed, why me?!

I want what you have
I want it to be easy
I want to shout at every accident and just wish it
was me.

It's not fair, that much I know
But I know its my journey.
I wear my badge with honour
In all that I've withstood..I know I'll be a mother.

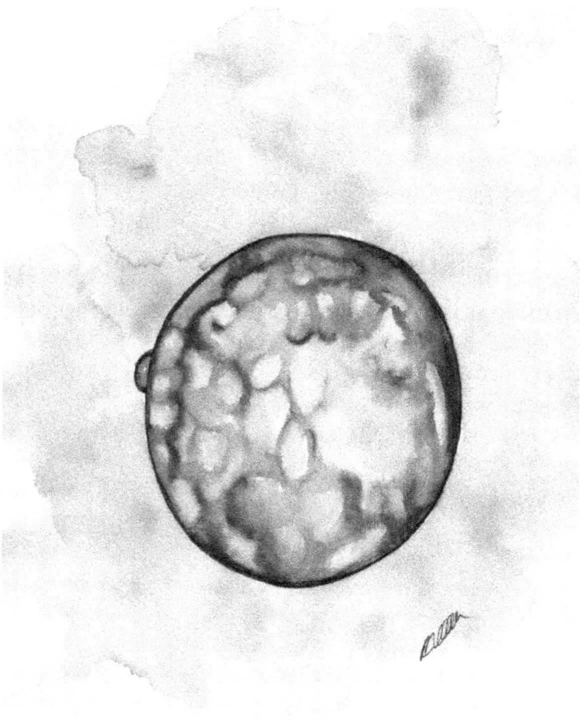

Unlike mine

Her body perfect, not yet weathered by years,
unlike mine.
Her skin so smooth, not yet touched from
becoming a mother, unlike mine.
Her breasts firm, unlike mine that nourished
another.
Her hair perfect in colour, unlike mine, Silver
with all the years I've pondered.
Her smile no lines to make me envy mine
Her hips are smooth, unlike mine that have
carried the fruit of our love.
A body to envy, unlike mine,
A body of memories,
A body that gave life,
A body that's lived a beautiful life;
A body to celebrate.

My old best friend

I mourned you like you died,
I missed you like no other;
Part of me died when
You said goodbye to this friendship.
It broke me;
I was struggling,
Stuck in my head,
Emotional and bruised and battered during the
journey to become a mother
I had no other.

Your words so cold;
Didn't you understand how much I wanted to be
a mother?
You told me to cancel all my plans;
Your words hurt me like no other,
I already felt like such a failure.
I felt I was never enough..it solidified my
decision.
Your expectations were too much!

Our lives on different paths;
Mine to have a family,
Yours to climb the ladder of success...
Two lives intertwined

Yet polar opposites repelling against one
another;
To slowly watch it collapse in such an
undignified manner.

I used all my spite..I spoke in anger..
I knew this could not recover.

I did my best to reconnect,
I forgave you for the words you said.

All those years you started walking from me;
As I feared,
You slipped away.
You stepped back until one day you
disappeared...
It happened so slowly
And all at once;
It was a painful blow
perfecty executed -
No arbitration needed.

Never another word was spoken;
The days turned to months the months to years
with no resolution.

I wish I knew what to say.
I wish to have one more conversation.
When I think of you, my old best friend,

I hope your life is blessed
With no regrets

I'm glad I knew you regardless of how it went;
I'm glad I'm free of the restrictions and all the
limitations I felt.

Thank you for leaving.
It allowed me to grow;
I became a better person,
I learnt valuable lessons.
Thank you for blessing me,
Thank you for the memories;
For that I'm always greatful.
We both said things that are regretful.
Perhaps one day we can put it to rest..
Until then, goodbye my old best friend.

Tiny beauty

A room full of strangers, white and sterile
without a comfort;
My body lay broken, unable to continue.
Completely defeated,
Numbness sets in,
Knife to skin;
The fear kicks in.
You look at me
Just as scared as I am.

Layer by layer,
Deeper and deeper,
I'm closer to you
The doubts arrive;
Will I be a good Mother?
Will I fail as a wife?
Will we make it through?
Panic sets in.
I can't bare anymore;
I'm about to break.

A small sound fills the room;
This tiny beauty, above the lights so bright
Her eyes so wide,
So pure, so untouched.

She was just apart of me
Now she is here.
Our eyes connect;
Relief falls upon me.

I waited a lifetime to see who you were
Now you're here and
You've all I've ever wanted
And yet I only just knew.
You're all I've ever wanted
My tiny beauty.

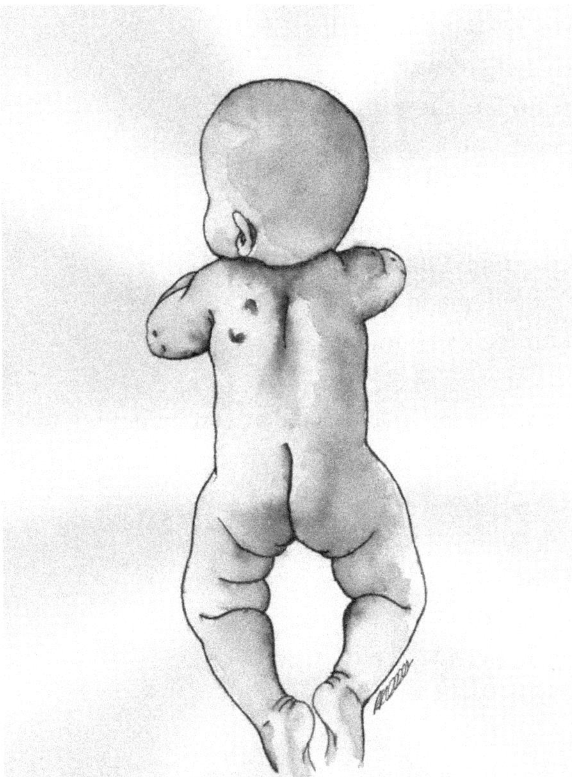

Cold

You push me and pull me in,
This tug of war;
Its no fair game -
I wish you knew how much this hurts.

Your love, so warm
And so inviting..
You pull me in
It all feels so enticing

I relish in the love and the affection, but not too long then you turn so uninviting

The coldness I feel
It hurts me,
It wounds me,
I'm left in a tail spin
Of feelings and rejection

Your love burns bright and I run to it... before you snuff it out
When you turn dark as night,
Your cheek cold
Turned from me

I'm in the dark wondering

Am I loved?
Am I enough?
Am I beautiful?
Or too much?

I'm cold again;
I'll blame myself -
And I'll wait until you light up again
And like a moth to a flame
I'll let myself be burnt again.

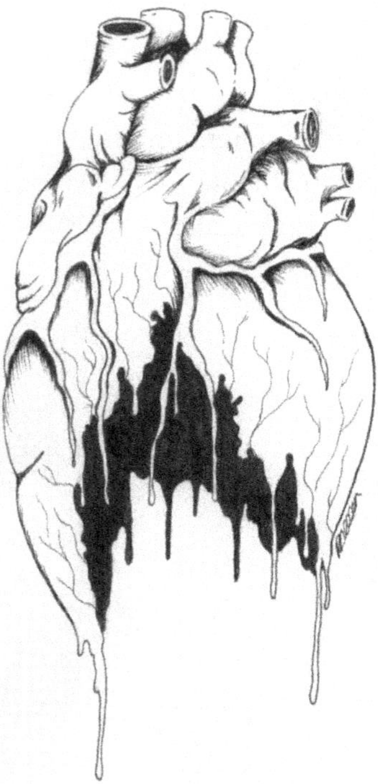

Darkness

The darkness, she creeps in;
she's here again.
The darkness is deep and unrelenting;
she's never gone;
she always lingers.
She's here again;
she's in my mirror,
she's in my head.
The darkness reminds me of all that I am not.
The darkness; unsatisfied, thirsty once more,
she comes for me to take me away.
She reminds me of how useless and pathetic I
am.
The darkness is brutal;
the darkness, is she right?
The darkness pushes me down...
I'm drowning; I have no fight.
The more I fight, the more she hurts me.
She feeds on me, delighting in my mercy.

Unable to scream, she silences me.
"Darkness, please stop!"
I scream, but make no sound -
her power, relentless.
I bow down as she consumes me.

The darkness is me and I am her.
The darkness has taken me once more.

Ocean

You say you love me,
You say you care,
You kiss me with your lies, bitter to taste.
The lies, the lies,
I hear what I want;
I'm blinded by the beauty of your face.

How can you love me
yet speak such spite?
What is this love if it shatters me apart?
I want to remove my beating heart.

I hate myself,
I hate how I love,
I hate that I care.
I want to stop feeling
Just end this now;
So many times you've left me here bleeding.

I beg to you be kind, end me now.
I can't look at you one more day.
You tell me you love me;
A false prophet, I am the fool
How can you love me?
Because I am the fool.

My heart calls to you like a siren to the sea.
Tomorrow I'll still love you,
Never knowing where I belong, lost in this ocean floating alone.

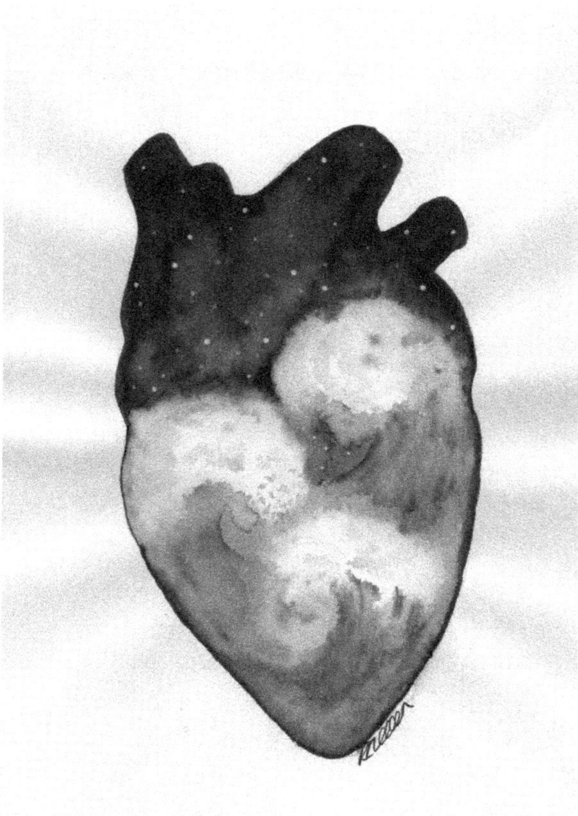

Poisoned land

Everything we tried to grow
Has turned to dust;
We took the land for granted,
Poisoned it with hate and mistrust.
Nothing grows here
Everything has died.
We live in a place of poison, void of life and
love;
A place between somewhere and nowhere,
A place of exile,
A place void of beauty,
A place that was once our paradise,
A place where your heart becomes dry,
A place where you feel no need, want, nor lust,
A place where tears become dust,
A place without love,
A place without trust,
A place without us.

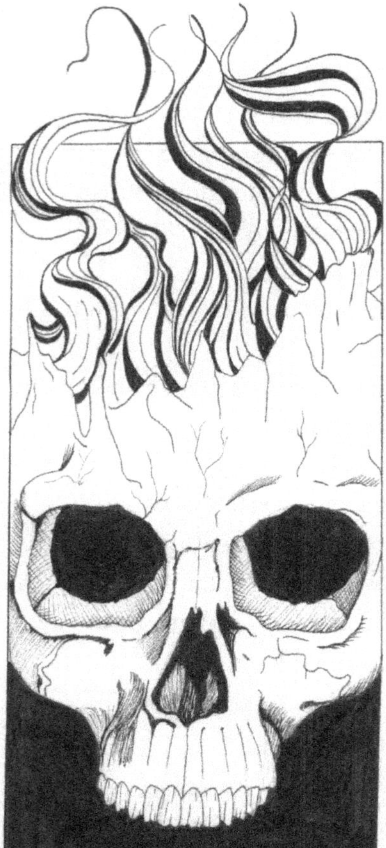

Ode to you

I'm lucky because you get me through.
So alike one another we are;
No thought too insane.
She runs away with me when life feels too hard.
She gets my emotions,
She loves my daughter like her own.
I'm so lucky to have you;
Your my sister,
My best friend,
My everything!
This is an ode to you -
The wonderful you -
Never thinking of yourself;
So selfless, so wonderful.
I hope I'm all the same things to you as you are to me.
This is an ode to the wonderful beautiful you.
Thank you.

Gemini

Born such a beauty,
So small, so fair;
Those early days
Filled with worry and fear.
So tiny, so fragile;
My smallest love.
Your eyes so wide
Full of wonder
Curiosity.

My littlest love
You are still the same;
Your curiosity and strongwill
Unlike another.

Your hair touched by fire,
Skin so perfect and pure,
Eyes so blue,
How can you be mine?

Your words so sweet,
Your mind so sharp,
My little Gemini,
How are you mine?

I watch you in admiration.
I hold you close when you are sleeping;
Those perfect fingers entwined with mine.

Her mind afire with tomorrow's delight;
Her excitement,
Her lust for life,
So enticing;
My bright and beautiful little love.

Seasons of you

Your words can be cold...
Colder and harsher than a winters day;
all my flowers have gone.

My hope has left me,
My beauty has disappeared.

The things you say burn me...
Like fire in the summer;
They set my whole world alight.

Your words cause me pain, and
I grieve the kindness you once spoke.

When your words are sweet and endearing, kind and welcoming,
I come to life;
the beauty inside me springs to life,
My colours flourish,
I start to bloom,
I'm drawn to you once again.

I know this moment won't last,
the summer, it turns back in to autumn..
The tears fall like the leaves,

And then,
The cold winter returns..to take me away again.

Broken Parts of me

You put me in this cage,
You show me the keys...
But I still remain within.

You lick your fingers, thumbing through the pages -
stopping past every mistake and regret.
You remind me of them in triumphant success.
A trophy of sorts -
First place... but it's no win
I cry
I scream
I die inside all over again
I rattle the cage; I wish to die.
You thumb through the catalogue
with distain, and it's my heart.

How can you love me
and torture me so?
How can you love me
and remind me of the worst parts of me?

I wish I was more to you than just a catalogue of all these broken parts.

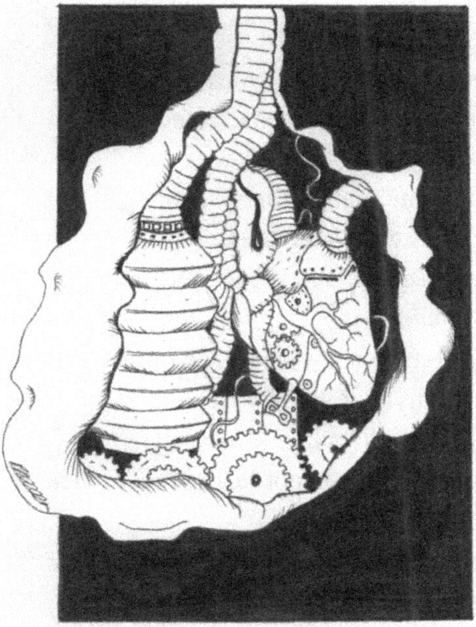

Mom

When I was little,
There was nothing like your hugs goodnight..
My fondest memories are of you reading fairy tales to me
And putting up the Christmas tree;
I relished in our moments together.

You taught me many things,
I always felt so loved and
You always did you best for me.
We never had money
I'm sure you wished you'd done more
But Mom, my childhood was
Perfect..I wouldn't change a thing.
You'd let me spin the pot lids in the kitchen always under your feet..
It never seemed a bother for you,
You took everything in your stride.

You let me wear your wedding dress 100 times..and use your one red lipstick.
I'd rummage through the glory box in awe of all your vintage clothes;
Your velvet pants and so much more...
I always wanted to be like you!

You never had much,
but you always gave!
Nothing was ever too much,
It always seemed so effortless;
I'm sure it wasn't,
So thank you
Because if there was ever a struggle, we didn't notice.
You were the perfect Mom
I know I talked alot,
The inquisitive kid with a big imagination..
Just like you, I dreamt away.
Thank you for every sacrifice and giving us a better life.
You've always been my best friend; my confidant...
You lavished me in love and affection, and I thank you for that for..
I love my daughter, how you loved me,
I do the same things you did with her as you did with me.

The Stars

"Tell me about the stars", she said..

"Tonight, they are bright in the sky and as I watch them, I think of you.
The moon, it's full like my love for you, the water calm as I feel today... I love you..I miss you."

"My love, what are the stars like tonight?" she asked.

"Tonight they are shining through clouds; the moon is waning and a cool breeze comes to push the clouds into view.
The reflection of the moon is shattered on the cold waters tonight; I feel so lonely."

"Oh my love, please tell me those stars are beautiful where you are?"

"My dear, I am in the darkness.
As I sit here, the moon is gone and the clouds are black.
I feel as if the world has swallowed me up; I'm in a belly of solitude.

The brightness has left me..
Tonight, my love,
I am lost.
I can't find my way back to you;
There are no stars tonight."

My love, my dearest love, where have you gone?
It's been night upon night without your mention of the stars; nothing is the same.
My love, my love, where have you gone? Please, I beg of you, come back and speak to me of our beautiful stars;
For nothing is the same.

Without you

I woke up to a new day without you;
I live in this world without you.
How unbearable it feels without you;
How cruel that I should be here without you.

A place without your laugh
A place without your smile
A place without your beauty
It feels no place at all.

Everyday reminded of you,
The want to speak to you
to ask a question, to never receive
To make a call, I cannot!
I miss your advice,
I miss our chatter,
The pain of it all; unbearable.

A place without you is no place at all,

Your home I miss you the most.

When I watch their little faces,
I see your smile, an expression..
so alike you..

a laugh
a glimmer
That felt like you came home.

You're here in them!
I'd been seeing it so wrong;
You never left;
you've always been here all along.

I'll miss you forever,
All that is true and
I'll speak your name
often so I feel close to you.
I'll keep your memory alive
Like you never left,
I'll keep your memory alive for them for us.

Cardigan

This cardigan, this fabric blue that touched your
skin now touches me;
it's all I have left of you.
This cardigan wraps around me like your hug
once did.
It gives me a moments peace to forget you've
gone.
This cardigan reminds me of you.
This cardigan is sombre, bitter sweet;
it reminds me of my sadness and things that
have gone..
A lifetime of memories no more to come.
This cardigan binds us in this moment, and
in this cardigan, I'm with you and feel
connected.
This cardigan is all I have of you;
this cardigan makes me reminiscent of you.
This cardigan is just woven threads, but it's so
much more than what you'd expect...
Your cardigan holds me and gives me hope to
see you again.
Your cardigan gives me strength to let go of
every regret, every word I wish I could unsend.

When I'm in your cardigan,
I re-live the beauty of the life you lived.

Running free

I never intended to feel so connected to you;
Four legs and hazel eyes,
Such a stubborn nature -
You kept me sane through it all.

The places we went,
The things we saw,
The love and loss we endured,
The hell we lived and the heaven we pursued...
You stayed by my side...
You - the Bonnie to my Clyde.

You'd been rescued from things I would never
know
With so many reasons to hate...
You were so kind to me and mine.
In your twilight years,
when you should have been resting,
you ran in pure delight.

Always happy in the company of the small one,
She intruded in your kennel and slept on you
But none of that ever bothered you.
Towards the end you got tired...
I saw you slowly slip from me
and all my fears

surfaced the day I had to say goodbye.

You departed this world...to meet me in the next.
It felt as if part of me died.
For 18 years, you were there for me
Throughout it all..

You were my company.
You licked away many tears,
Sat with me through it all.
If anything, you understood me best of all.
When I think of all we accomplished…
Your love was the easiest.

Thank you for choosing me,
My best friend.

www.ingramcontent.com/pod-product-compliance
Lightning Source LLC
Chambersburg PA
CBHW051735130826
49812CB00033B/875
* 9 7 8 9 3 5 7 2 1 3 1 6 5 *